CLD

SPANISH

AT A GLANCE

PHRASE BOOK & DICTIONARY FOR TRAVELERS

BY HEYWOOD WALD, Ph.D.
Former Chairman, Department of Foreign Languages
Martin Van Buren High School, New York

Third Edition

BARRON'S

ACKNOWLEDGMENTS

We would like to thank the following individuals and organizations for their assistance on this project: Patricia Brooks, author, *Fisher's Guide to Spain and Portugal*; René Campos, Director, Spanish Institute, New York City; Mercedes Garcia-Rodriguez, Spanish Institute, New York City; George Lange, George Lang, Inc., New York City; Professor Robert Piluso, SUC New Paltz, NY; Professor Henry Urbanski, Chairman, Department of Foreign Languages, SUC New Paltz, NY; Pilar Vico, Spanish National Tourist Office, New York City; Professor Lynn Winget, Wichita State University, KS; Herta Erville; Fernando Pfannl; Alfonso Hernández.

Also, the Association of American Travel Writers; *The New York Times*; *Signature* magazine; the Spanish Institute; the Spanish National Tourist Office; *Travel-Holiday* magazine; *Travel and Leisure* magazine; U.S. Tour Operators; and U.S. Travel Data Center.

All inquiries should be addressed to:
Barron's Educational Series, Inc.
250 Wireless Boulevard
Hauppauge, New York 11788
http://www.barronseduc.com

Library of Congress Catalog Card No. 99-80141

International Standard Book No. 0-7641-1257-0

Book Design Milton Glaser, Inc.
Illustrations Juan Suarez

PRINTED IN HONG KONG
9 8 7 6

CONTENTS

PREFACE

So you're taking a trip to one of the many fascinating countries of the world. That's exciting! This phrase book, part of Barron's popular *At a Glance* series, will prove an invaluable companion.

In these books we present the phrases and words that a traveler most often needs for a brief visit to a foreign country, where the customs and language are often different. Each phrase book highlights the terms particular to that country, in situations that the tourist is most likely to encounter. This new edition includes dialogues using words and expressions for each situation. Travel tips found throughout the book have been updated. With a specially developed key to pronunciation, this book will enable you to communicate quickly and confidently in colloquial terms. It is intended not only for beginners with no knowledge of the language, but also for those who have already studied it and have some familiarity with it.

Some of the unique features and highlights of the Barron's series are:

- Easy-to-follow *pronunciation keys* and complete phonetic transcriptions for all words and phrases in the book.
- Compact *dictionary* of commonly used words and phrases—built right into this phrase book so there's no need to carry a separate dictionary.
- Useful phrases for the *tourist*, grouped together by subject matter in a logical way so that the appropriate phrase is easy to locate when you need it.
- Special phrases for the *business traveler*, including banking terms, trade and contract negotiations, and secretarial services.
- Thorough section on *food and drink*, with comprehensive food terms you will find on menus.
- *Emergency phrases* and terms you hope you won't need: legal complications, medical problems, theft or loss of valuables, replacement or repair of watches, camera, etc.
- *Sightseeing itineraries*, with shopping tips, practical travel tips, and regional food specialties to help you get off the beaten path and into the countryside, to the small towns and cities, and to the neighboring areas.
- A *reference section* providing important signs, conversion tables, holidays, abbreviations, telling time, days of week, and months of year.
- A brief *grammar section*, with the basic elements of the language quickly explained.

Enjoy your vacation and travel with confidence. You have a friend by your side.

Travel Tips   There are many theories on how to survive jet lag—the adjustment to a long trip into a different time zone. Some multinational corporations take jet lag so seriously that they do not allow employees to make business decisions on the first day abroad. Most experts agree on several techniques: Eat lightly for several days before departing, avoid dehydration while flying by drinking plenty of nonalcoholic liquids; take frequent strolls around the plane to keep your blood circulating; if possible, get some rest on the flight; use ear plugs, an eye mask, and an inflatable neck collar to make sleep easier. If you arrive early in the morning, take an after-lunch nap, get up for some exercise and dinner, then go to bed at the regular new time. If you arrive at your destination in the afternoon or later, skip the nap and try to sleep late the next morning. In countries where massage or saunas are standard hotel service, indulge yourself on the evening of arrival to help you sleep soundly that night.

QUICK PRONUNCIATION GUIDE

Although all the phrases in this book are presented with an easy-to-use key to pronunciation, you will find speaking Spanish quite a bit easier if you learn a few simple rules. Many letters in Spanish are pronounced approximately as they would be in English. There are some differences, however, which are given below. Since these sounds rarely vary, you can follow these guidelines in pronouncing all Spanish words.

Spanish contains four additional letters not found in English: *ch, ll, ñ,* and *rr.* All letters are pronounced, with the exception of *h;* the letters *v* and *b* are most often both pronounced like the English *b.* Words ending in a vowel, an *n,* or an *s* are stressed on the next-to-last syllable—**casa** *(KAH-suh).* Words ending in a consonant (other than *n* or *s*) are stressed on the last syllable—**general** *(hehn-eh-RAHL).* A written accent is required on any words that break either of these rules—**lápiz** *(LAH-pees).*

Note: When pronouncing the words in the following examples, stress the vowels that appear in CAPITAL letters.

VOWELS

SPANISH LETTER(S)	SOUND IN ENGLISH	EXAMPLES
a	ah (y<u>a</u>cht)	taco *(TAH-koh)*
e	ay (d<u>ay</u>)	mesa *(MAY-sah)*
	eh (p<u>e</u>t)	perro *(PEH-roh)*
i	ee (m<u>ee</u>t)	libro *(LEE-broh)*
o	oh (<u>o</u>pen)	foto *(FOH-toh)*
u	oo (t<u>oo</u>th)	mucho *(MOO-choh)*

COMMON VOWEL COMBINATIONS (DIPHTHONGS)

SPANISH LETTER(S)	SOUND IN ENGLISH	EXAMPLES
au	ow (c<u>ow</u>)	causa *(COW-sah)*
		auto *(OW-toh)*
ei	ay (d<u>ay</u>)	aceite *(ah-SAY-tay)*
ai	y (t<u>y</u>pe)	baile *(BY-lay)*
ie	yeh (<u>ye</u>t)	abierto *(ah-BYEHR-toh)*
ue	weh (<u>we</u>t)	bueno *(BWEH-noh)*

CONSONANTS

SPANISH LETTER(S)	SOUND IN ENGLISH	EXAMPLES
c (before *a, o, u*)	hard k sound (<u>c</u>at)	campo *(KAHM-poh)*
		cosa *(KOH-sah)*
		Cuba *(KOO-bah)*
c (before *e, i*)	soft s sound (<u>c</u>ent)	central *(sehn-TRAHL)*
		cinco *(SEEN-koh)*
cc	hard and soft cc (ks sound) (a<u>cc</u>ept)	acción *(ahk-see-OHN)*
ch	hard ch sound (<u>ch</u>air)	muchacho *(moo-CHAH-choh)*
g (before *a, o, u*)	hard g (<u>g</u>o)	gafas *(GAH-fahs)*
		goma *(GOH-mah)*
g (before *e, i*)	breathy h (<u>h</u>ot)	general *(hehn-eh-RAHL)*
h	always silent	hasta *(AHS-tah)*
j	breathy as in h sound (<u>h</u>ot)	José *(ho-SAY)*
l	English l sound (<u>l</u>amp)	lámpara *(LAHM-pahr-ah)*
ll	as in English y (<u>y</u>es)	pollo *(POH-yoh)*
n	English n (<u>n</u>o)	naranja *(nah-RAHN-ha)*
ñ	English ny (can-<u>y</u>on)	señorita *(seh-nyoh-REE-tah)*
qu	English k (<u>k</u>eep)	que *(kay)*
r	trilled once	caro *(KAH-roh)*

SPANISH LETTER(S)	SOUND IN ENGLISH	EXAMPLES
rr (or r at beginning of word)	trilled strongly (operator, three)	rico (*RREE-koh*) perro (*PEH-rroh*)
s	English s (<u>see</u>)	rosa (*ROH-sah*)
v	Approximately as in English b (<u>b</u>ook)	primavera (*pree-mah-BEHR-ah*)
x	English s, ks (<u>s</u>ign, so<u>cks</u>)	extra (*ES-trah*) examinar (*ek-sah-mee-NAHR*)
y	English y (<u>y</u>es) (by itself y = i)	yo (*yoh*) y (*ee*)
z	English s	zapato (*sah-PAH-toh*)

The above pronunciations apply to the Spanish that is spoken in Central and South America, and that is also spoken in parts of southern Spain. The remaining areas of Spain use the Castilian pronunciation, which differs mostly in the sound of the letters *ll* and of the *z* and the *c* before *e* and *i*. For example, the Castilian pronunciations are as follows:

SPANISH LETTER(S)	SOUND IN ENGLISH	EXAMPLES
ll	ly sound as in million	llamo (*LYAH-moh*)
c (before *e* or *i*)	a <u>th</u> sound instead of an s sound	gracias (*GRAH-thee-ahs*)
z		lápiz (*LAH-peeth*)

THE BASICS FOR GETTING BY

MOST FREQUENTLY USED EXPRESSIONS

The following are expressions you'll use over and over—
the fundamentals of polite conversation, the way to express
what you want or need, and some simple question tags that
you can use to construct all sorts of questions. We suggest
you become very familiar with these phrases.

Hello!	**¡Hola!**	*OH-lah*
Yes	**Sí**	*see*
No	**No**	*noh*
Maybe	**Quizás**	*kee-SAHS*
Please	**Por favor**	*pohr-fah-BOHR*
Thank you (very much).	**(Muchas) gracias.**	*(MOO-chahs) GRAH-see-ahs*
You're welcome.	**De nada.**	*day NAH-dah*

Excuse me

- (having disturbed or bumped into someone) — **Perdón** *pehr-DOHN*
- (leaving a group or walking in front of a person) — **Con permiso** *kohn pehr-MEE-soh*
- (getting one's attention) — **Por favor** *pohr fah-BOHR*

I'm sorry.	**Lo siento.**	*loh see-EHN-toh*

Just a second.	**Un momento.** *oon moh-MEN-toh*
That's all right, okay.	**Está bien.** *eh-STAH bee-ehn*
It doesn't matter.	**No importa.** *noh eem-PORT-ah*
Good morning.	**Buenos días.** *bway-nohs DEE-ahs*
Good afternoon.	**Buenas tardes.** *bway-nahs TAHR-dehs*
Good evening (night).	**Buenas noches.** *bway-nahs NOH-chehs*
Sir	**Señor** *seh-NYOHR*
Madame	**Señora** *seh-NYOHR-ah*
Miss	**Señorita** *seh-nyohr-EE-tah*
Good-bye.	**Adiós.** *ah-DYOHS*
See you later (so long).	**Hasta la vista (Hasta luego).** *AH-stah lah BEE-stah (AH-stah loo-AY-goh)*
See you tomorrow.	**Hasta mañana.** *AH-stah mah-NYAH-nah*

COMMUNICATIONS

Do you speak English?	**¿Habla usted inglés?** *ah-blah oos-TEHD een-GLAYS*
I speak (a little) Spanish.	**Hablo español (un poco).** *AH-bloh ehs-pah-NYOHL (oon POH-koh)*
I don't speak Spanish.	**No hablo español.** *noh AH-bloh ehs-pah-NYOHL*

Is there anyone here who speaks English?	**¿Hay alguien aquí que hable inglés?** *AH-ee AHL-ghee-ehn ah-KEE kay AH-blay een-GLAYS*
Do you understand?	**¿Comprende usted?** *kohm-PREHN-day oos-tehd*
I understand.	**Yo comprendo.** *yoh kohm-PREHN-doh*
I don't understand.	**No comprendo.** *noh kohm-PREHN-doh*
What? What did you say?	**¿Cómo?** *KOH-moh*
How do you say ____ in Spanish?	**¿Cómo se dice ____ en español?** *KOH-moh say DEE-say ____ ehn ehs-pah-NYOHL*
What do you call this (that) in Spanish?	**¿Cómo se llama esto (eso) en español?** *KOH-moh say YAH-mah EHS-toh (EHS-oh) ehn ehs-pahn-YOHL*
Please speak slowly.	**Hable despacio, por favor.** *AH-blay dehs-PAH-see-oh pohr fah-BOHR*
Please repeat.	**Repita, por favor.** *ray-PEE-tah pohr fah-BOHR*

INTRODUCTIONS

I'm American (English) (Australian) (Canadian).	**Soy norteamericano(a), (inglés, inglesa), (australiano, australiana), (canadiense).** *soy nohr-tay-ah-mehr-ee-KAH-noh (nah) (een-GLAYS een-GLAY-sah) (ow-strahl-YAH-noh nah) (kah-nah-DYEHN-say)*
My name is ____.	**Me llamo ____.** *may YAH-moh*

What's your name?	**¿Cómo se llama usted?**	*KOH-moh say YAH-mah oos-TEHD*
How are you?	**¿Cómo está usted?**	*KOH-moh ehs-TAH oos-TEHD*
How's everything?	**¿Qué tal?**	*kay tahl*
Very well, thanks. And you?	**Muy bien, gracias. ¿Y usted?**	*mwee bee-EHN GRAH-see-ahs ee oos-TEHD*

GETTING AROUND

Where is ____?	**¿Dónde está ____?**	*DOHN-day ehs-TAH*
the bathroom	**el baño**	*ehl BAH-nyoh*
the bus stop	**la parada de autobuses**	*lah pahr-AH-dah day ow-tow-BOOS-ehs*
the dining room	**el comedor**	*ehl koh-meh-DOHR*
the entrance	**la entrada**	*lah ehn-TRAH-dah*
the exit	**la salida**	*lah sahl-EE-dah*
the subway	**el metro**	*ehl MEH-troh*
the taxi stand	**la parada de taxis**	*lah pah-RAH-dah day TAHK-sees*
the telephone	**el teléfono**	*ehl tehl-EHF-oh-noh*
the train station	**la estación de trenes**	*lah esh-tah-SYOHN day TREH-nehs*
I'm lost.	**Me he perdido.**	*may heh pehr-DEE-doh*
We're lost.	**Nos hemos perdido.**	*nohs HEH-mohs pehr-DEE-doh*
Where are ____?	**¿Dónde están ____?**	*dohn-day ehs-TAHN*

I am looking ____.	**Busco ____.** *BOOS-koh*
to the left	**a la izquierda** *ah lah ees-kee-EHR-dah*
to the right	**a la derecha** *ah lah dehr-EH-chah*
straight ahead	**derecho** *deh-REH-choh*

SHOPPING

How much is it?	**¿Cuánto es?** *KWAHN-toh ehs*
	¿Cuánto vale? *KWAHN-toh BAH-lay*
I'd like ____.	**Quisiera ____.** *kee-see-YEHR-ah*
Please bring me ____.	**Tráigame, por favor ____.** *TRAH-ee-gah-may pohr fah-BOHR*
Please show me ____.	**Muéstreme, por favor ____.** *MWEHS-treh-may pohr fah-BOHR*
Here it is.	**Aquí está.** *ah-KEE eh-STAH*

MISCELLANEOUS

I'm hungry.	**Tengo hambre.** *TEHN-goh AHM-bray*
I'm thirsty.	**Tengo sed.** *tehn-goh SEHD*
I'm tired.	**Estoy cansado (m.) Estoy cansada (f.)** *eh-stoy kahn-SAH-doh (dah)*
What's that?	**¿Qué es eso?** *kay ehs EHS-oh*
What's up?	**¿Qué hay?** *kay AH-ee*
I (don't) know.	**Yo (no) sé.** *yoh (noh) say*

QUESTIONS

Where is (are) ____?	**¿Dónde está (están) ____?**	*DOHN-day eh-STAH (STAHN)*
When?	**¿Cuándo?**	*KWAHN-doh*
How?	**¿Cómo?**	*KOH-moh*
How much?	**¿Cuánto?**	*KWAHN-toh*
Who?	**¿Quién?**	*key-EN*
Why?	**¿Por qué?**	*pohr KAY*
Which?	**¿Cuál?**	*kwal*
What?	**¿Qué?**	*kay*

EXCLAMATIONS, SLANG, COLLOQUIALISMS

Ouch!	**¡Ay!**	*AH-ee*
Wow! Gosh! (surprise) or Darn it! (annoyance)	**¡Caramba!** *kah-RAHM-bah* **¡Caray!** *kah-RAH-ee*	
How pretty!	**¡Qué bonito! (m.)** *kay boh-NEE-toh* **¡Qué bonita! (f.)** *kay boh-NEE-tah*	
That's awful!	**¡Es horrible!**	*ehs ohr-EE-blay*
Great! Wonderful!	**¡Estupendo!** *ehs-too-PEHN-doh* **¡Magnífico!** *mahg-NEE-fee-koh* **¡Fenomenal!** *feh-noh-meh-NAHL*	
That's it!	**¡Eso es!**	*ehs-oh EHS*
My goodness!	**¡Dios mío!**	*dyohs MEE-oh*
Good Heavens!	**¡Cielos!**	*see-YEH-lohs*

Bottoms up, cheers.	**¡Salud!**	*sah-LOOD*
Quiet!	**¡Silencio!**	*see-LEHN-see-oh*
Shut up!	**¡Cállese!**	*KAH-yeh-say*
That's enough!	**¡Basta!**	*BAHS-tah*
Never mind!	**¡No importa!**	*noh eem-POHR-tah*
Of course!	**¡Claro!**	*KLAH-roh*
With pleasure.	**¡Con mucho gusto!**	*kohn MOO-choh GOOS-toh*
Let's go!	**¡Vamos!**	*BAH-mohs*
What a shame (pity)!	**¡Que lástima!**	*kay LAH-stee-mah*
What a nuisance! (showing annoyance)	**¡Qué lata!**	*kay LAH-tah*
Good luck!	**¡(Buena) suerte!**	*bweh-nah SWEHR-tay*

PROBLEMS, PROBLEMS, PROBLEMS (EMERGENCIES)

Watch out!	**¡Cuidado!**	*kwee-DAH-doh*
Hurry up!	**¡Dése prisa!**	*day-say PREE-sah*
Look!	**¡Mire!**	*MEE-reh*
Listen!	**¡Escuche!**	*ehs-KOO-cheh*
Wait!	**¡Espere!**	*ehs-PEHR-eh*
Fire!	**¡Fuego!**	*FWAY-goh*

ANNOYANCES

What's the matter with you?	**¿Qué le pasa?** *kay lay PAH-sah*
What (the devil) do you want?	**¿Qué (diablos) quiere usted?** *kay (dee-AH-blohs) kee-EHR-eh oos-TEHD*
Stop bothering me!	**¡No me moleste más!** *noh meh moh-LEHS-tay mahs*
Go away!	**¡Váyase!** *BAH-yah-say*
Leave me alone!	**¡Déjeme en paz!** *DAY-heh-meh ehn PAHS*
Help, police!	**¡Socorro, policía!** *soh-KOH-roh poh-lee-SEE-yah*
I'm going to call a cop!	**¡Voy a llamar a un policia!** *boy ah yah-MAHR ah oon pohl-ee-SEE-yah*
That guy is a thief!	**¡Ese tipo es un ladrón!** *ehs-eh tee-poh ehs oon lah-DROHN*

He has stolen ____.	**Me ha robado ____.** *may ah roh-BAH-doh*
my car	**el coche** *ehl KOH-chay*
my passport	**el pasaporte** *ehl pah-sah-POHR-tay*
my purse	**la bolsa** *lah BOHL-sah*
my suitcase	**la maleta** *lah mahl-EH-tah*
my wallet	**la cartera** *lah kahr-TEHR-ah*
my watch	**el reloj** *ehl ray-LOH*

This young man is annoying me.	**Este joven me esta molestando.** *ehs-teh HOH-behn may ehs-TAH moh-lehs-TAHN-doh*
He keeps following me.	**Me está siguiendo.** *may ehs-TAH see-ghee-YEHN-doh*
Stop that boy!	**¡Paren a ese muchacho!** *PAH-rehn ah ehs-eh moo-CHAH-choh*

COMPLICATIONS

I haven't done anything.	**Yo no he hecho nada.** *yoh noh eh EH-choh NAH-dah*
It's a lie!	**¡Es mentira!** *ehs mehn-TEE-rah*
It's not true.	**No es verdad.** *noh ehs behr-DAHD*
I'm innocent.	**Soy inocente.** *soy een-oh-SEHN-teh*
I want a lawyer.	**Quiero un abogado.** *kee-YEHR-oh oon ah-boh-GAH-doh*
I want to go ____.	**Quiero ir ____.** *kee-YEHR-oh eer*
to the American (British) (Australian) (Canadian) Consulate	**al consulado norteamericano (inglés), (australiano), (canadiense)** *ahl kohn-soo-LAH-doh nohr-tay-ah-mehr-ee-KAH-noh (een-GLAYS) (ow-strahl-YAH-noh) (kah-nah-DYEHN-say)*

to the police station	**al cuartel de policía** *ahl kwahr-TEHL day poh-lee-SEE-ah*
I need help, quick.	**Necesito ayuda, pronto.** *nehs-ehs-EE-toh ah-YOO-dah PROHN-toh*
Can you help me, please?	**¿Puede usted ayudarme, por favor?** *pweh-day oos-TEHD ah-yoo-DAHR-may pohr fah-BOHR*
I have lost ____.	**He perdido ____.** *ay pehr-DEE-doh*
Does anyone here speak English?	**¿Hay alguien aquí que hable inglés?** *AHl-ee AHL-ghee-yehn ah-KEE kay AH-blay een-GLEHS*
I need an interpreter.	**Necesito un intérprete.** *neh-seh-SEE-toh oon een-TEHR-preh-tay*

NUMBERS

You will use numbers the moment you land, whether it be to exchange money at the airport, purchase a bus ticket for a ride into town, or describe the length of your stay to a customs official. We list here first the cardinal numbers, then follow with ordinal numbers, fractions, and other useful numbers.

CARDINAL NUMBERS

0	**cero**	*SEHR-oh*
1	**uno**	*OO-noh*
2	**dos**	*dohs*
3	**tres**	*trehs*
4	**cuatro**	*KWAH-troh*
5	**cinco**	*SEEN-koh*
6	**seis**	*sayss*
7	**siete**	*SYEH-tay*
8	**ocho**	*OH-choh*
9	**nueve**	*NWEH-bay*
10	**diez**	*dyehs*
11	**once**	*OHN-say*
12	**doce**	*DOH-say*
13	**trece**	*TREH-say*
14	**catorce**	*kah-TOHR-say*
15	**quince**	*KEEN-say*

16	**diez y seis (dieciséis)** *dyeh-see-SAYSS*
17	**diez y siete (diecisiete)** *dyeh-see-SYEH-tay*
18	**diez y ocho (dieciocho)** *dyeh-see-OH-choh*
19	**diez y nueve (diecinueve)** *dyeh-see-NWEH-bay*
20	**veinte** *BAYN-tay*
21	**veintiuno** *bayn-tee-OO-noh*
22	**veintidós** *bayn-tee-DOHS*
23	**veintitrés** *bayn-tee-TREHS*
24	**veinticuatro** *bayn-tee-KWAH-troh*
25	**veinticinco** *bayn-tee-SEEN-koh*
26	**veintiséis** *bayn-tee-SAYSS*
27	**veintisiete** *bayn-tee-SYEH-tay*
28	**veintiocho** *bayn-tee-OH-choh*
29	**veintinueve** *bayn-tee-NWEH-bay*
30	**treinta** *TRAYN-tah*
40	**cuarenta** *kwahr-EHN-tah*
50	**cincuenta** *seen-KWEHN-tah*
60	**sesenta** *seh-SEHN-tah*
70	**setenta** *seh-TEHN-tah*
80	**ochenta** *oh-CHEHN-tah*

90	**noventa** *noh-BEHN-tah*
100	**cien(to)** *syehn(toh)*
101	**ciento uno** *SYEHN-toh OO-noh*
102	**ciento dos** *SYEHN-toh DOHS*
200	**doscientos (as)** *dohs-SYEHN-tohs (tahs)*
300	**trescientos (as)** *trehs-SYEHN-tohs (tahs)*
400	**cuatrocientos (as)** *kwah-troh-SYEHN-tohs (tahs)*
500	**quinientos (as)** *kee-NYEHN-tohs (tahs)*
600	**seiscientos (as)** *sayss-SYEHN-tohs (tahs)*
700	**setecientos (as)** *seh-teh-SYEHN-tohs (tahs)*
800	**ochocientos (as)** *oh-choh-SYEHN-tohs (tahs)*
900	**novecientos (as)** *noh-beh-SYEHN-tohs (tahs)*
1.000	**mil** *meel*
2.000	**dos mil** *dohs meel*
1.000.000	**un millón** *oon mee-YOHN*
2.000.000	**dos millones** *dohs mee-YOHN-ays*

Note: In Spanish, thousands are separated by periods, not commas.

ORDINAL NUMBERS

first	**primero (primer, -a)**	*pree-MEH-roh (rah)*
second	**segundo (a)**	*seh-GOON-doh (dah)*
third	**tercero (tercer,-a)**	*tehr-SEH-roh (rah)*
fourth	**cuarto (a)**	*KWAHR-toh (tah)*
fifth	**quinto (a)**	*KEEN-toh (tah)*
sixth	**sexto (a)**	*SEHS-toh (tah)*
seventh	**séptimo (a)**	*SEHT-tee-moh (mah)*
eighth	**octavo (a)**	*ohk-TAH-boh (bah)*
ninth	**noveno (a)**	*noh-BAY-noh (nah)*
tenth	**décimo (a)**	*DEH-see-moh (mah)*
last	**último (a)**	*OOL-tee-moh (mah)*
once	**una vez**	*OO-nah behs*
twice	**dos veces**	*dohs BEH-sehs*
three times	**tres veces**	*trehs BEH-sehs*

FRACTIONS

half of ____.	**la mitad de ____.**	*lah mee-TAHD day*
▪ half (of) the money	**la mitad del dinero**	*lah mee-TAHD del dee-NEH-row*
half a ____.	**medio ____.**	*MEH-dyoh*
▪ half a kilo	**medio kilo**	*MEH-dyoh KEE-loh*
a fourth (quarter)	**un cuarto**	*oon KWAHR-toh*

a dozen ____.	**una docena de ____.** *OO-nah doh-SAY-nah day*
a dozen oranges	**una docena de naranjas** *OO-nah doh-SAY-nah day nah-RAHN-hahs*
100 grams	**cien gramos** *syehn GRAH-mohs*
200 grams	**doscientos gramos** *dohs-SYEHN-tohs GRAH-mos*
350 grams	**trescientos cincuenta gramos** *trey-SYEHN-tohs seen-KWEHN-tah GRAH-mos*
a pair (of) ____.	**un par de ____.** *oon pahr day*
a pair of shoes	**un par de zapatos** *oon pahr day sah-PAH-tohs*

QUANTITIES

I want ____.	**Quiero ____.** *KEE-eh-roh*
a bag of	**una bolsa de** *OO-nah BOHL-say day*
a bottle of	**una botella de** *OO-nah boh-TEH-yah day*
a box of	**una caja de** *OO-nah KAH-hah day*
a can of	**una lata de** *OO-nah LAH-tah day*
a dozen of	**una docena de** *OO-nah doh-SEH-nah day*
a kilo of	**un kilo de** *oon KEE-loh day*
a liter of	**un litro de** *oon LEE-troh day*
a package of	**un paquete de** *oon pah-KEH-teh day*
a pair of	**un par de** *oon PAHR day*
a pound of	**una libra de** *OO-nah LEE-brah day*

a slice of	**una tajada de** *OO-nah tah-HA-dah day*
a bit of	**un poco de** *oon POH-ko day*
a lot of	**mucho** *MOO-choh*
enough of	**suficiente** *soo-fee-SYEHN-tay*
too much	**demasiado** *deh-mah-SYAH-doh*

WHEN YOU ARRIVE

PASSPORT AND CUSTOMS

Customs is usually a routine procedure in Spain. Items that can be brought in duty-free include clothing, jewelry, and personal effects needed for a visit; 200 cigarettes or 50 cigars; 2 liters of wine or 1 liter of spirits (above 22 percent alcohol); 1/4 liter of cologne.

For personal use, you may bring in one of each: still camera with 10 rolls of film; video camera; a portable radio; typewriter; binoculars; bicycle; musical instrument; record player; pocket calculator; tape recorder; cassette player. Also, you may bring unlimited foreign currency, travelers checks, and Spanish pesetas. Amounts exceeding 1 million pesetas must be declared on entry. No more than 1 million pesetas may be exported.

Customs in other Spanish-speaking countries vary greatly, although crossing the border into Mexico is usually a very casual affair. We suggest you check ahead, should you be entering any country in Central or South America.

My name is ____.	**Me llamo ____.** *may YAH-moh*
I'm American (British) (Australian) (Canadian).	**Soy norteamericano(a), (inglés, a), (australiano, a), (canadiense).** *soy nohr-tay-ah-mehr-ee-KAH-noh(nah) (een-GLAYS ah) (ow-strahl-YAH-noh nah) (kah-nah-DYEHN-say)*
My address is ____.	**Mi dirección es ____.** *mee dee-rehk-SYOHN ehs*
I'm staying at ____.	**Estoy en el hotel ____.** *ehs-TOY ehn ehl oh-TEHL*
Here is (are) ____.	**Aquí tiene ____.** *ah-KEE TYEHN-ay*
▪ my documents	**mis documentos** *mees doh-koo-MEHN-tohs*

▥ my passport	**mi pasaporte**	*mee pah-sah-POHR-tay*
▥ my tourist card	**mi tarjeta de turista**	*mee tahr-HAY-tah day toor-EES-tah*
I'm ____.	**Estoy ____.**	*ehs-TOY*
▥ on a business trip	**en un viaje de negocios**	*ehn oon bee-AH-hay day neh-GOH-see-ohs*
▥ on vacation	**de vacaciones**	*day bah-kah-SYOHN-ays*
▥ visiting relatives	**visitando a mis familiares**	*bee-see-TAHN-doh ah mees fah-meel-YAHR-ays*
▥ just passing through	**solamente de paso**	*soh-lah-MEHN-tay day PAH-soh*
I'll be staying here ____.	**Me quedaré aquí ____.**	*may kay-dahr-AY ah-KEE*
▥ a few days	**unos días**	*OON-ohs DEE-ahs*
▥ a few weeks	**unas semanas**	*OON-ahs seh-MAH-nahs*
▥ a week	**una semana**	*OON-ah seh-MAH-nah*
▥ a month	**un mes**	*oon mehs*
I'm traveling ____.	**Viajo ____.**	*bee-AH-hoh*
▥ alone	**solo(a)**	*SOH-loh(lah)*
▥ with my husband	**con mi marido**	*kohn mee mah-REE-doh*
▥ with my wife	**con mi mujer**	*kohn mee moo-HAIR*
▥ with my family	**con mi familia**	*kohn mee fah-MEEL-yah*
▥ with my friend	**con mi amigo(a)**	*kohn mee ah-MEE-go(ah)*

Customs in the major ports of entry is a simple affair. As you pass through the gates, you'll see signs dividing the path in two directions: Follow the green arrow if you have nothing to declare (**nada que declarar**), or head for the red arrow if you have items to declare (**artículos para declarar**).

NADA QUE DECLARAR	**ARTICULOS PARA DECLARAR**

These are my bags.	**Estas son mis maletas.** *EHS-tahs sohn mees mah-LAY-tahs*
I have nothing to declare.	**No tengo nada que declarar.** *noh tehn-goh NAH-dah kay day-klahr-AHR*
I only have ____.	**Sólo tengo ____.** *SOH-loh tehn-goh*
▪ a carton of cigarettes	**un cartón de cigarrillos** *oon kahr-TOHN day see-gahr-EE-yohs*
▪ a bottle of whisky	**una botella de whisky** *OON-nah boh-TEH-yah day WEE-skee*
What's the problem?	**¿Hay algún problema?** *AH-ee ahl-GOON proh-BLAY-mah*
They're gifts (for my personal use).	**Son regalos (para mi uso personal).** *sohn ray-GAH-lohs (pah-rah mee OO-soh pehr-sohn-AHL)*
Do I have to pay duty?	**¿Tengo que pagar impuestos?** *ten-goh kay pah-GAHR eem-PWEHS-tohs*
May I close my bag now?	**¿Puedo cerrar la maleta ahora?** *pweh-doh sehr-AHR lah mah-LEH-tah ah-OHR-ah*

IDENTITY CARD (TARJETA DE IDENTIDAD)

Upon entering the country (or on your flight into the country), you will be required to complete an identity card, usually with the following information.

Apellidos: (Surname) _____

Nombre: (First Name) _____

Nacionalidad: (Nationality) _____

Fecha de nacimiento: (Date of Birth) _____

Profesión: (Profession) _____

Dirección: (Address) _____

Pasaporte expedido en: (Passport Issued in) _____

BAGGAGE AND PORTERS

   You will find carts for your baggage at virtually all airports.
After you have retrieved your bags, push your cart through
the "Nothing to Declare" doors. After customs, you can carry
your bags to the taxi or bus stand—or ask a porter for help.
Porters are readily available.

Where can I find a baggage cart?	**¿Dónde está un carrito para-maletas?** *DOHN-day eh-STAH oon kahr-REE-toh pah-rah mah-LEH-tahs*
I need a porter!	**¡Necesito un maletero!** *neh-seh-SEE-toh oon mah-leh-TEH-roh*

These are our (my) bags.	**Estas son nuestras (mis) maletas.** *EHS-tahs sohn NWEHS-trahs (mees) mah-LEH-tahs*
▦ that big (little) one	**esa grande (pequeña)** *EH-sah GRAHN-day (peh-KAYN-yah)*
▦ these two black (green) ones	**estas dos negras (verdes)** *EHS-tahs dos NEH-grahs (BEHR-days)*
Put them here (there).	**Póngalas aquí (allí).** *POHN-gah-lahs ah-KEE (ah-YEE)*
Be careful with that one!	**¡Cuidado con ésa!** *kwee-DAH-doh kohn EH-sah*
I'll carry this one myself.	**Yo me llevo ésta.** *yoh may YEH-boh EHS-tah*
I'm missing a suitcase.	**Me falta una maleta.** *may FAHL-tah oo-nah mah-LEH-tah*
How much do I owe you?	**¿Cuánto le debo?** *KWAHN-toh lay DEHB-oh*
Thank you (very much). This is for you.	**(Muchas) gracias. Esto es para usted.** *(moo-chahs) GRAHS-yahs EHS-toh ehs pah-rah oos-TEHD*

AIRPORT TRANSPORTATION

Where can I get a taxi?	**¿Dónde puedo tomar un taxi?** *DOHN-deh PWEH-doh toh-MAHR oon TAHK-see*
How much is the taxi ride into the city?	**¿Cuánto cuesta el viaje en taxi a la ciudad?** *KWAHN-toh KWEHS-tah ehl BYAH-heh ehn TAHK-see ah lah see-yoo-DAHD*
What buses go into the city?	**¿Qué autobuses van a la ciudad?** *KAY ow-toh-BOOS-ehs bahn ah lah see-you-DAHD*

Where is the bus stop?	**¿Dónde está la parada del autobús?** *DOHN-deh ehs-TAH lah pah-RAH-dah del ow-toh-BOOS*
How much is the fare?	**¿Cuánto cuesta el viaje?** *KWAHN-toh KWEHS-tah ehl BYAH-heh*
Where can I rent a car?	**¿Donde puedo arrendar un coche?** *DOHN-deh PWEH-doh ah-ren-DAHR oon KOH-cheh*

Travel Tips There was a time when buying an airline ticket was simple. Since the airline industry was deregulated, however, travelers must shop and compare prices, buy charter or discount tickets far in advance and join frequent flier clubs to become eligible for free tickets. Read the fine print in ads and ask questions when making reservations. Often, discount fare tickets cannot be exchanged for cash or another ticket if travel plans must be changed. If you must change plans en route, talk to an airline ticket agent. Sometimes they have soft hearts!

BANKING AND MONEY MATTERS

The **peseta** is the currency of Spain, with 100 **céntimos** in each **peseta.** Best exchange rates are usually offered at banks, of which there are dozens. Banco Exterior has an office at the airport in Madrid.

No later than July 2002, the *euro*, the new European monetary currency, will replace all bank notes and national currencies of the countries that are members of the European Community. The euro will be divided in cents and will be issued in the following denominations: notes—5, 10, 20, 50, 100, 200, and 500; coins—1, 2, 5, 10, 20, 50 cent, 1 and 2 euro.

In Mexico and many countries in Central and South America, the **peso** is the currency, with 100 **centavos** equaling one peso. In recent years, devaluations and value fluctuations have had profound effects on the peso's exchange value. You will get a very favorable exchange for pounds or dollars.

Major credit cards are widely accepted, as are all major travelers checks.

Banking hours are generally from 9 A.M. to 3 P.M., Monday through Friday, plus Saturday morning. Business hours are usually from 9 A.M. to 1:30 P.M., then 4:30 P.M. to 8 P.M., Monday through Friday. Many businesses keep Saturday morning hours too. "Morning" in Spain or Mexico generally means until it is time for the lunch break—i.e., 1 or 1:30 P.M.

CURRENCIES OF
SPANISH-SPEAKING COUNTRIES

Argentina	**peso**	*PEH-soh*
Bolivia	**peso**	*PEH-soh*
Chile	**peso**	*PEH-soh*
Colombia	**peso**	*PEH-soh*
Costa Rica	**colón**	*koh-LOHN*